MW01611524

CCO FAITH STUDY SERIES

PARTICIPANT GUIDE

DISCOVERY

Discovery Participant Guide

Created and published by Catholic Christian Outreach Canada. 2nd edition. Copyright © 2020. All rights reserved.

Nihil Obstat: Patrick Fletcher, Ph.D. *Censor Deputatus*

Imprimatur: ✠Terrence Prendergast, S.J. *Archbishop of Ottawa* July 31, 2018 *Feast of St. Ignatius of Loyola*

Catholic Christian OUTREACH

501-1400 St. Laurent Boulevard
Ottawa, ON K1K 4H4
Canada

Phone: 613-736-1999
faithstudies@cco.ca
cco.ca

Printed in Canada.
ISBN: 978-1-928144-98-4

The cover image chosen for *Discovery* is a sunrise. It represents our desire for the person and presence of Jesus to be unveiled and discovered in the hearts of all. *Discovery* participates in the mission of St. John the Baptist:

'And you, child, will be called the prophet of the Most High;
* for you will go before the Lord to prepare his ways,*
to give knowledge of salvation to his people
* by the forgiveness of their sins.*
By the tender mercy of our God,
* the dawn from on high will break upon us,*
to give light to those who sit in darkness and in the shadow of death,
* to guide our feet into the way of peace.'*
Luke 1:76-79

The people who walked in darkness
* have seen a great light;*
those who lived in a land of deep darkness —
* on them light has shined.*
Isaiah 9:2

To St. Ignatius of Loyola and St. Francis Xavier
who longed for the name of Jesus
to be proclaimed and exalted the world over.

Table of Contents

DISCOVERY Small Group Information

TIME:

PLACE:

LEADER:

   PHONE NUMBER:

   EMAIL:

PARTICIPANTS:

LESSON 1

God's Love

Introduction

Christian faith is built upon the love of God. God's love is the central message of Christianity and the source of our faith. We need to understand God's love if we are to make sense of anything else the Catholic Church professes.

The expression "God loves you" is familiar to many—so familiar, in fact, that we risk forgetting what it means. If we were to ask at a Christian gathering who thinks God loves them, the majority of people would likely raise their hands. One has to wonder, though, do we *really* know God loves us?

Many people think of God's love in general, vague or detached terms; their experience of it is thus rather thin, shallow and impersonal. Surely, if God is God, his love should give us much more than a vague sense of comfort. It *must* be more than this.

1 **What happens in our hearts when we are loved? How are we affected?**

God's Personal Love

God's love for us is personal, proven, merciful and offered. We will look at these aspects of God's love throughout this faith study. It is important to understand all of them in order to appreciate the true character of God's love for us. It can be difficult to believe that God loves us as individuals and knows and cares about our personal lives. The truth is that he knows each of us by name. He knows all the details of our lives, even to the number of hairs on our heads! He loves us and delights in us individually. We need to hear these truths.

2 Write down what strikes you about God's personal love in these passages:

JEREMIAH 29:11

ISAIAH 49:15-16

PSALM 139:1-3

God's Secure Love

3 Write down the qualities of God's love expressed in the following passages:

JOHN 10:10-15

ROMANS 8:35, 37-39

4 How would you describe God's love in light of these reflections, Scripture verses, and any personal experiences?

Our Personal Love for God

We may find it hard to believe that God loves us personally. This is perhaps because we relate to him in an impersonal way, thinking of him as a faraway cosmic entity. Because we don't believe he is personal or accessible, we treat him in a detached and distant kind of way.

5 **How would we relate to God if we considered him as a Person (as a close friend)?**

6 **Read Matthew 18:2-3. How might we relate to God if we approached him with a childlike heart?**

Summary

God's love for us is very real. *Discovery* will look at how God's love is personal, proven, merciful and offered. In this first lesson, we have focused on God's personal love; his care and concern for each human being is central to our Christian faith. We are invited to be secure in his intimate, unchanging, eternal and unconditional love.

Living It Out

CHALLENGE
Choose one way to relate to God as someone who is personally present in your life.

MEMORIZE JEREMIAH 29:11
For surely I know the plans I have for you, says the Lord, plans for your welfare and not for harm, to give you a future with hope.

LESSON 2

Love's Initiative

1 Discuss how last week's challenge went.

Introduction

Last week, we focused on God's personal love for us. He knows our names and every detail of who we are. In today's lesson, we will begin to look at how God's love is proven, merciful and offered. God's love is good news for our lives. Before we can truly appreciate this news, however, we must understand why it is so good and why we need it.

Love is Offered

The Book of Genesis tells us that God created everything in the heavens and the earth out of nothing, and that everything he created was good. The world reflects his beauty, creativity and glory. The crown of his creation was man and woman. In the creation narrative, we are told that in the middle of the garden of Eden there was a tree—the "tree of the knowledge of good and evil." This was the only tree in the garden from which Adam and Eve were forbidden to eat. We know the rest of the story: Adam and Eve were tempted by the serpent and ate the fruit from the tree. This was the original sin.

2 Read Genesis 3:1-7. We learned last week that God's love is unconditional, personal and secure, so there must be a loving reason why he would put one tree in the garden from which Adam and Eve were not to eat. How is this consistent with who God is?

An Offer You Can Refuse

God's love is freely offered. We *can* refuse it. The story of Adam and Eve shows us, however, that refusing God's love is a rejection of what will bring us joy and fulfillment.

3 **What attitudes, beliefs or misconceptions were at the root of Adam and Eve's choice to disobey?**

Adam and Eve chose to disobey God's directives, not trusting that his way would lead them to fulfillment. Regrettably, what they found outside of God's plan was separation, shame and death (Genesis 3). In order to genuinely understand the good God offers, we should take a moment to look at the unfortunate effects that turning away from him (sin) has on our lives.

4 **Read Isaiah 59:2. How does sin affect our relationship with God?**

5 Read Romans 5:12. What is another consequence of sin?

Love is Proven

When we turn away from God's commandments and his love, we hurt him, ourselves and others. Despite our turning away, however, God never stops loving us. As in any great love story, God, the protagonist, pursues us to win us back.

6 Think of someone who loves you. What assures you of this person's love?

7 Read Romans 5:6-8. How does God prove his love for us?

Love is Merciful

The parable of the Prodigal Son paints a moving picture of the Father's love for us. The young man who squanders his inheritance is called "prodigal" because the word means rash, wasteful or recklessly extravagant. Prodigal can also be used in a positive sense, however, to describe extravagant generosity. In this case, the father too is prodigal. This parable shows us how God the Father proves his extravagant love for us, despite our turning away from him.

8 **Read Luke 15:11-24. The father agrees to give the son his inheritance. What does this say about the father's character?**

9 **Why do you suppose the son wanted to leave?**

10 What did the son do with his freedom?

11 What were the results of his actions?

12 Why did the son decide to return home?
How has his view of home changed?

13 What is significant about the father's response to his son's return?

14 Consider how intense and immediate the father's forgiveness was. What does this say to you about our Heavenly Father's love, mercy and forgiveness?

Summary

God never imposes his love on us, nor forces us to love him in return—we are free to choose him and the life he offers us. Sin is choosing that which can hurt God, others and ourselves. Even when we sin, however, our Heavenly Father shows his love for us; he patiently waits for us to turn back to him. He proved his love by sending his Son to make a way for us to be reconciled; "For God so loved the world that he gave his only Son, so that everyone who believes in him may not perish but may have eternal life" (John 3:16).

Living It Out

CHALLENGE

Go to Mass this week with an attentive mindset, with humble sorrow for your failures and joyful anticipation of the Father's welcome and all that his house has to offer. Listen carefully to all the readings and prayers to catch their depth of meaning. Be prepared to share with your group next week something that stood out for you in a fresh way at Mass.

MEMORIZE ROMANS 5:8

But God proves his love for us in that while we still were sinners Christ died for us.

LESSON 3

Jesus Christ— Our Lord

1 **Share how last week's challenge went.**

Introduction

You may have heard Jesus referred to as Lord and Saviour. These terms each describe a unique aspect of Jesus' identity. It is important to understand each separately before we can grasp how they complement one another. Today we will look at Jesus as Lord.

Christianity is unique among world religions, because it emphasizes more than just moral teachings and a way of life. It hinges on the identity of Jesus Christ, who was truly God and truly man.

I believe in one Lord Jesus Christ,
the Only Begotten Son of God,
born of the Father before all ages.
God from God, Light from Light,
true God from true God,
begotten, not made,
consubstantial with the Father;
through him all things were made.
For us men and for our salvation
he came down from heaven,
and by the Holy Spirit
was incarnate of the Virgin Mary,
and became man.
THE NICENE CREED

Recognizing Jesus' identity is essential to the Christian faith. If the man—Jesus of Nazareth—is not also God, then the Christian faith is utterly demolished.

Is the Bible a reliable source?

For the remainder of this lesson we will look at a number of selections from the Bible in which Jesus claims to be God or to have attributes ascribed only to God. However, before we can establish the divinity of Christ from the Bible, we need to ask if the Bible is a reliable source of historical information. Two of the most common questions asked about the Bible are:

a) Does the Bible faithfully express the meaning of its original authors, or has its message been changed over the centuries?

b) Do the Gospels accurately reflect what Jesus actually said and did?

One way to establish the legitimacy of ancient documents is to examine manuscripts from as close as possible to the original time they were written. You may be surprised to learn that the New Testament is the most documented work of ancient literature, with over 5000 more ancient manuscripts still in existence compared to its closest competitor. With this vast collection of manuscripts, scholars have been able to trace the accuracy of the copies of the New Testament that have been passed down, and have found that the oldest manuscripts are 97-99% identical. Therefore, we can say with strong certainty that the New Testament in your hands today accurately reflects what was written by the First Century authors.

Let us now wrestle with Jesus' most controversial and remarkable claim: his divinity.

The Divinity of Christ

Jesus caused controversy and curiosity wherever he went because of his powerful words and miracles. He left everyone wondering, "Who is this man?" or even, "Who does this man think he is?"

The Gospel writers give us an account of society's attitudes and opinions about Jesus during his public ministry and his Passion—from the Pharisees, to the crowds, to his disciples, to the Romans, and even to the demons. Jesus was seen as a great man, a miracle worker, a superb moral teacher and perhaps Israel's hope for freedom from Roman tyranny. More importantly, many understood that he claimed to be equal with God, and for this scandalous blasphemy, the Chief Priests sought to kill him.

Scripture does not describe an occasion when Jesus said the words "I am God." However, a careful look at the Gospels shows that Jesus claimed equality with God, especially by taking upon himself attributes only God could possess.

We will look at a number of Scripture selections in which Jesus claims to be God or have attributes ascribed only to God. As we go through the passages, refer to the list of divine descriptions below.

A. Son of Man	G. the truth
B. the way to eternal life	H. equal with God
C. the authority to forgive sins	I. the Christ/the Messiah
D. gives life	J. Son of God
E. one with the Father	K. deserving the same honour as God
F. the authority to judge	L. "I Am"

2 John 8:51-59. How does Jesus claim to be God?

3 How does Jesus astound the Jews in this passage?

4 Luke 5:20-26. How does Jesus claim to be God?

5 Mark 14:61-64. How does this passage reaffirm the claims made in the last two Scripture selections?

6 John 4:25-26. How does Jesus identify himself to the woman?

7 John 5:21-23. What divine attributes does Jesus give himself in this Scripture passage?

8 John 10:24, 30-33. What is the conflict described in this Scripture narrative?

9 John 14:6-7. What are the claims to divinity in these verses?

10 What truths are embedded in the words *the way, the truth, the life*?

The Trilemma

Many people would consider Jesus to be a great moral teacher but find it difficult to believe that Jesus was divine.

However, as we have seen, Jesus repeatedly equated himself with God. This leads us into an argument called the *Trilemma*, which puts forward three possibilities regarding his claim to be God. His claim can only be true or false; someone cannot claim to be God and be both right and wrong at the same time. If his claim is false, then either Jesus lied about his identity, or he was sincerely deluded. Or, his claim to be God was true.

There is much reasonable and practical evidence to suggest that Jesus is not a liar nor deluded, but Lord.

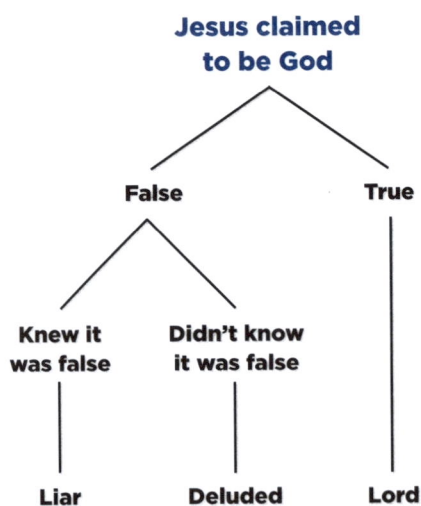

Option #1: Jesus lied

The first objection to this argument is that Jesus claimed to be God, but he knew he was not—in other words, he lied.

11 **What are some characteristics you would associate with a liar?**

12 **Are these characteristics exhibited by Jesus?**

Option #2: Jesus was deluded

What if Jesus genuinely thought he was God, but he was wrong? Could it be that Jesus was simply deluded about his claim of divinity?

13 **What are some characteristics you would associate with someone who suffered from a delusion that they were God?**

14 **Are these characteristics exhibited by Jesus?**

Option #3:
Jesus is who he says he is—God

As we have seen in this lesson, the Gospels clearly depict that Jesus claimed to be God on numerous occasions. His enemies acknowledged that he claimed to be God when they charged him with blasphemy. When his claim was challenged under the threat of execution, he did not equivocate or retract his claim. Even when it was clear that he was to be found guilty of blasphemy and executed, Jesus stood firm in his divine identity.

15 What divine characteristics are exhibited by Jesus?

In a quiet moment with his disciples, Jesus asked them a question: "Who do people say that I am?" The disciples respond with a few options: John the Baptist, Elijah, or one of the other prophets. Then Jesus asks them for their opinion: "But who do you say that I am?" (Mark 8:27-29). Today, this same question is posed to you. You have seen how the Gospels recount Jesus' claim to be divine. You have seen the possible answers to the question of whether or not Jesus is God. Now, the question is yours to answer: who do you say that Jesus is? Is he a liar, is he deluded, or is he Lord and God?

Summary

No serious scholars dispute the historical existence of Jesus of Nazareth. He is widely considered to be a great moral teacher. In reading the Gospels, however, we discover that Jesus never intended to be perceived as simply a moral teacher. He repeatedly equated himself with God. No other respected figure in history, no other founder of the world's great religions, has made such claims. The entire Christian faith hinges on this fundamental claim.

Living It Out

CHALLENGE

This week, seriously consider whether or not you believe Jesus is telling the truth when he says that he is God.

MEMORIZE JOHN 14:6

I am the way and the truth and the life. No one comes to the Father except through me.

Jesus Christ— Our Saviour

1 Discuss how last week's challenge went.

Introduction

Last week, we looked at the divinity of Jesus—Jesus as Lord. Now we will look at what it means to say that Jesus is our Saviour. We will see the ultimate way in which Jesus, as Saviour, proves God's merciful love for each of us.

2 What kind of things did Jesus do during his public ministry on earth?

3 What do you think was Jesus' main reason for being on earth?

Bridging Earth to Heaven

To help us better understand Jesus as Saviour, we will look at insights from St. Catherine of Siena, a Doctor of the Church. In her writings she shares a visual description of salvation which God revealed to her.

St. Catherine describes Adam and Eve and how they were created in God's image. In Eden, they tasted the beginnings of communion with God that would have grown as they spiritually matured, so that eventually, they would have fully known his eternal goodness, tenderness and love.

However, sin created irreparable problems; it caused an impassable division between God and man. St. Catherine describes this separation as a great, raging river that made it absolutely impossible for man to reach God, as much as man might try. This impassable, powerful river of sin leads to death. The picture painted at this point is very bleak indeed.

4 **In light of this description and what you have already learned in Lesson 2, what are the results of sin?**

God the Father deals with the problem of sin by sending his Son into the world. Through his death on the cross, Jesus becomes a bridge so that we can reach heaven.

> So I gave you a bridge, my Son, so that you could cross over the river, the stormy sea of this darksome life, without being drowned....And how foolish to choose to drown rather than accept the remedy I have given!...And why should he have made of himself a roadway? So that you might in truth come to the same joy as the angels.
>
> *St. Catherine of Siena: The Dialogue*, p. 58-59

> For in him all the fullness of God was pleased to dwell, and through him God was pleased to reconcile to himself all things, whether on earth or in heaven, by making peace through the blood of his cross.
>
> Colossians 1:19-20

5 **How did Jesus' death on the cross deal with the problems sin created?**

JOHN 1:29

ROMANS 6:23

2 CORINTHIANS 5:18-19

6 Read Romans 5:16-19. In light of these Scripture verses and the bridge illustration, why was humanity in need of God's help? In other words, why did we need Jesus to die for us?

7 Jesus' death and resurrection restores our relationship with God. What prevents us from grasping how necessary Jesus is?

So far in the analogy, the bridge is in place but humanity and God remain separated. We have not yet crossed the chasm. In the next lesson, we will discuss why it is important to God—and vital for us—that we make it across the bridge to God's side.

Summary

Jesus Christ is the revelation of God's love and mercy. His love is capable of rescuing each of us from slavery to sin and death.

> " He alone makes it possible for every human person to share eternal life. "
>
> St. Pope John Paul II,
> *Message for World Mission Sunday 2005.*

Living It Out

CHALLENGE

Share the bridge analogy with someone this week.

MEMORIZE ROMANS 6:23

For the wages of sin is death, but the free gift of God is eternal life in Christ Jesus our Lord.

LESSON 5

Love is Offered

1 **Discuss how last week's challenge went.**

Introduction

Let's start things off this week with a big question, probably the biggest you will ever face.

Dr. Peter Kreeft is a respected professor of Philosophy at Boston College. During his many years of teaching at this Catholic university, he has asked many students the thought-provoking question: *"If you were to die tonight and God asked you, 'Why should I let you into heaven?', what would you say?"*

2 **What do you think most people in the class said?**

Back At The Bridge

In last week's cliffhanger, we are left reflecting on how we will get to the other side of the bridge.

3 How do we actually cross that bridge? See Acts 2:36-38 and Romans 10:9 to verify your answers.

4 Now how would you answer the question, "Why should I let you into heaven?"

The Relationships Diagram

Over the past four lessons, we have looked at the personal, merciful and proven love of God. We discussed how very intimately God knows each and every one of us. We have seen the Father's heart of mercy, which welcomes us back from our wanderings. Fully God, Jesus left heaven and became man to prove his love for us, even to the point of dying on the cross for our sins. This merciful God *offers* his love to all of us; he invites us individually to make his love our heart's home.

The following illustration helps us to identify how we are living our relationship with Jesus. It also helps us to understand the kind of relationship he desires to have with us: a relationship of friendship, intimacy, commitment, fidelity, mercy and love.

OUTSIDE OF MY LIFE

PART OF MY LIFE

CENTRE OF MY LIFE

OUTSIDE OF MY LIFE

PART OF MY LIFE

CENTRE OF MY LIFE

The top three images represent levels of commitment in three kinds of human relationships. The dashes around the person represent various aspects of this person's life, such as career, school, family, recreation, etc. The first image represents someone who is single; there is no romantic relationship in this person's life. The second image represents someone who is dating; this relationship is part of this person's life, but commitment is limited. The third image represents someone who is married; there is an intimate relationship and a permanent mutual commitment.

Let's compare this to our relationship with God.

The bottom three images represent levels of commitment in a relationship with God. The first image represents someone who does not have a relationship with Jesus and considers Jesus to be outside his or her life. The second image represents someone who acknowledges Jesus as part of his or her life, but has not completely committed to him. Jesus is just one aspect of this person's life among many others. The third image represents a Christ-centred relationship. This relationship is primary and central, influencing all decisions and every aspect of this person's life.

5 In light of this diagram, how do you think a person begins or recommits to a relationship with Jesus?

Starting a relationship with Jesus is much like exchanging marriage vows. You begin by saying "yes" or "I do" to Jesus. You ask him to be part of your life, in good times and in bad, and you commit yourself to him. For those who have been baptized, it is making an adult faith decision to affirm what our parents chose for us at our Baptisms.

A Christ-centred life is a life of discipleship: living in relationship and friendship with Jesus. It is a life of forgiveness, healing, freedom, hope, love and comfort in difficult times. Christ is rightfully honoured when he is at the centre of our lives because it acknowledges his supreme greatness when we recognize him as Lord and Saviour.

As we consider this invitation and decision to live with Christ at the centre of our lives, we might encounter some interior concerns and doubts. *What will this decision mean for me? Can I really live out such a commitment?*

6 What might be holding you back from a Christ-centred life?

Next we will look at some common barriers and misconceptions when considering Christ's invitation to relationship.

Scale of Perfection

A common barrier is the misconception that the relationship diagrams show a scale of spiritual perfection. This attitude can often be attributed to the mistaken belief that being in a relationship with Jesus is about "measuring up" or mastering the Christian life. We think the relationships diagram is an assessment of how "spiritual" we are. We assume that only perfect people like St. Teresa of Calcutta could really be in the Christ-centred relationship.

We can feel uncomfortable to even consider claiming to be in a Christ-centred relationship. We may think it would be too arrogant, and that it would be more humble to say our commitment is represented by the second image or somewhere between the second and third image.

The relationships diagram is emphasizing commitments we make (whether consciously or not), not degrees of spiritual perfection. Although living our faith is essential to our relationship with God, the person in the second kind of relationship with God is not necessarily less "religious" than the person in the Christ-centred relationship. The defining question is one of commitment. *Who is at the centre of my life? To whom am I entrusting my life?*

7 At first glance, what do you think is the difference between the person who sees their commitment to God represented by the second image and the person who would say it is like the third image?

Let's go back to Dr. Kreeft's question to help our understanding of a relationship with Christ.

8a In light of the scenario presented by Dr. Kreeft, how would a person in the second kind of relationship answer the question about why God should let them into heaven?

8b What would the person in the Christ-centred relationship say?

Think back to the story of the Prodigal Son in Lesson 2. When the son returned to say that he was "no longer worthy to be called your son," his father did not ask him to correct all his faults before he offered his forgiveness. Instead, the father was filled with compassion and ran to embrace him. Similarly, when we make the decision to turn our hearts to God, he does not demand perfection before he offers his forgiveness; he is filled with compassion and runs to embrace us.

Fear of Failure

A second barrier we encounter is related to self-doubt. We aren't sure we can live up to what God expects of us.

We need to know that though our failures are inevitable, Jesus will not fail us. We fear that if we fail, God will abandon us; we must remember that God's love is unconditional, as we learned in Lesson 1. We can also look to the example of human relationships as an analogy of how we can relate to God.

9a How would a prevailing fear of failure affect a relationship with a friend?

9b How would a fear of failure similarly affect the way we relate to Jesus?

10 Read Hebrews 13:5. What encouragement can we take in light of any fear of failure?

Fear of Change

The decision to invite Christ to be at the centre of our lives is certainly a life-changing decision. It is a decision to orient our whole life, our life's actions, choices, priorities and purpose toward God. This means making some choices to change the way we are living, so as to honour God and live as a follower of Jesus. There are other fears about allowing Christ to be at the centre of our lives. We can worry about the changes this kind of decision will impose on our current way of life.

11 What are the kinds of changes people might fear about inviting Christ to be at the centre of their lives?

> If we let Christ into our lives, we lose nothing, nothing, absolutely nothing of what makes life free, beautiful and great. No! Only in this friendship are the doors of life opened wide. Only in this friendship is the great potential of human existence truly revealed.... Dear young people: do not be afraid of Christ! He takes nothing away and he gives you everything. When we give ourselves to him, we receive a hundredfold in return. Yes, open, open wide the doors to Christ—and you will find true life.
>
> Pope Benedict XVI
> *Mass for the Inauguration of his Pontificate*

12 What do you think might need to change in your life if you embrace a Christ-centred relationship? Take a moment to reflect and write down potential changes in your life.

Universal Invitation— Personally Yours

We have just looked at various obstacles when considering a Christ-centred relationship. God knows our fears and weaknesses, and doesn't expect us to be instantly perfect. He is with us to help us every step of the way. Be assured that God greatly desires to be in a right and restored relationship with each of us, with *you*. Jesus Christ has made the way possible through his life, death and resurrection.

> Finally, I turn to every man and woman, including those who have fallen away from the Church, who have left the faith or who have never heard the proclamation of salvation. To everyone the Lord says: "Behold, I stand at the door and knock; if anyone hears my voice and opens the door, I will come in to him and eat with him, and he with me" (Revelation 3:20).
>
> *Verbum Domini,* 124

In Jewish culture, to share a meal is a sign of welcoming and intimacy—a powerful sign of what is happening between us and Jesus. In the classic painting based on Revelation 3:20 by William Holman Hunt, Jesus is portrayed knocking at a door which has no handle. This door can only be opened from the inside. Jesus will come in if *we* open the door to him. Do you hear him knocking? Will you open the door to Christ?

What are the obstacles to a Christ-centred relationship that you need to take to prayerful reflection this week?

The decision to put Christ at the centre of your life is perhaps the most important decision you will ever make. Jesus is offering you his everlasting love and forgiveness, and all he asks for in return is your love and your faith in him. A decision like this should not be taken lightly, and so we want to give you space to reflect on your answer to the question:

Which of the three relationships do you want to represent your relationship with Jesus?

Your *Discovery* leader will set up a time to meet with you personally before Lesson 6 to discuss your response to this most important question.

Summary

What an incredible love story! God proved his love for us by sending his Son to die on the cross to reconcile us with himself. For love to truly be love it has to be offered and received. In Christ we are offered love, reconciliation and the hope of eternal life. He invites us to make that choice through faith and to reorient our lives, placing God at the centre of all we do, becoming his disciples.

Living It Out

CHALLENGE

This week, prayerfully consider Christ's invitation to relationship. Ask yourself: "What might be holding me back from this decision?" Plan a time to meet individually with your small group leader sometime this week to discuss your response to Christ's invitation to a personal relationship.

MEMORIZE REVELATION 3:20

Listen! I am standing at the door, knocking; if you hear my voice and open the door, I will come in to you and eat with you, and you with me.

LESSON 6

A New Life

1 **Share what you thought about last week's lesson.**

Introduction

Over the course of *Discovery*, we've been unpacking the richness of the Good News. Like pieces of a puzzle, the truths about Jesus have come together so that we can clearly grasp the beauty and scope of God's plan for our salvation. Last week we saw that the last piece of the puzzle is ourselves. Christ desires to be at the centre of our lives and he gives us the freedom to invite him in as our true Lord and our Saviour. We are choosing to become his disciple—his follower.

Review

Over the past five lessons, *Discovery* has outlined the basic message of the Catholic faith, often referred to as the *kerygma*, a Greek word that means to cry or proclaim as a herald. The *kerygma* is the message the Church has proclaimed from its very beginning, and includes these four key points:

1. God created every person to have a personal relationship with him.

2. Our relationship with God has been broken through our sins.

3. Jesus restores our relationship with God through his death and resurrection (known as the Paschal Mystery).

4. God invites us to this restored relationship; each person responds to this invitation by choosing a Christ-centred life.

The *Catechism of the Catholic Church* provides a summary of the *kerygma* in its first paragraph.

> **"** God, infinitely perfect and blessed in himself, in a plan of sheer goodness freely created man to make him share in his own blessed life. For this reason, at every time and in every place, God draws close to man. He calls man to seek him, to know him, to love him with all his strength. He calls together all men, scattered and divided by sin, into the unity of his family, the Church. To accomplish this, when the fullness of time had come, God sent his Son as Redeemer and Savior. In his Son and through him, he invites men to become, in the Holy Spirit, his adopted children and thus heirs to his blessed life. **"**
>
> *Catechism of the Catholic Church*, 1

Let's look at how this section of the *Catechism* outlines the basic message of the *kerygma*.

2 How does this section of the *Catechism* describe:

That we are created for a relationship with God?

The consequences of sin?

The solution to the problem of sin?

Our relationship with God if we accept the gift of salvation offered in Jesus?

Personal Encounter

 Conversion means accepting, by a personal decision, the saving sovereignty of Christ and becoming his disciple.

St. John Paul II
Redemptoris Missio, 46

A conversion of life happens when we make a personal decision to invite Christ to be at the centre of our lives. This invitation is personal and we can expect to have a personal encounter with God. This might be a powerful experience, or it might be a delicate one. Although we won't know God fully and completely until we are in Heaven, we can certainly experience him in our lifetime. He desires for us to know him. If you want to experience him more, ask him!

 Describe a personal experience you have had of God's presence.

4 How could you make yourself more available and open to God so as to encounter, know and love him better?

Personal Prayer

Prayer is an essential part of nurturing our relationship with God. Taking time each day to pray enables us to continually recognize our need for Christ and to commit ourselves to him. Our time of personal prayer does not have to be complicated—in fact, it is a lot like talking to a close friend.

5 What would be a good plan for you to make sure you pray and talk to Jesus every day?

Communal Encounter

We have emphasized the unique personal encounter we can have with Jesus. This is very real and beautiful, but it's not all. Yes, we are personally known and valued by God, and at the same time we are united to all who are baptized in Christ. As children of God, we are brothers and sisters in the family of God, which is the Church.

> **"** He [God] calls man to seek him, to know him, to love him with all his strength. He calls together all men, scattered and divided by sin, into the unity of his family, the Church....He invites all men to become, in the Holy Spirit, his adopted children and thus heirs to his blessed life. **"**
>
> *Catechism of the Catholic Church*, 1

As the family of God we are a community of believers who share a love for the Saviour. This is one reason we gather in churches, have liturgies and serve together in ministry. God's plan for us is not only an individual encounter. As the quote above notes, God has called everyone into "the unity of his family," which is the Church. He desires for us to gather and publicly worship and serve together as the Church, the Body of Christ.

1 CORINTHIANS 12: 12-13A

6 **What are some examples of communal expressions of faith?**

7 **How can our communal expressions of faith enhance our personal relationship with God?**

Communal Prayer

There are many ways we can pray together as a community of faith. One of the most significant ways we pray together as a Church happens annually at every Easter Vigil Mass all over the world. In a solemn and special way, we renew our baptismal promises. Our response is a personal "I do"—but we all say it *together*. This is a powerful affirmation of how our faith is both *individual* and *communal*.

As we wrap up *Discovery* we will make this same personal and communal proclamation of faith. We will renew our baptismal promises together as a small group, just like we do at the Easter Vigil.

+ **Do you reject sin, so as to live in the freedom of God's children?**
  R. I do

+ **Do you reject the glamour of evil, and refuse to be mastered by sin?**
  R. I do

+ **Do you reject Satan, father of sin and prince of darkness?**
  R. I do

+ **Do you believe in God, the Father almighty, creator of heaven and earth?**
  R. I do

+ **Do you believe in Jesus Christ, his only Son, our Lord, who was born of the Virgin Mary, was crucified, died, and was buried, rose from the dead, and is now seated at the right hand of the Father?**
  R. I do

+ **Do you believe in the Holy Spirit, the holy catholic Church, the communion of saints, the forgiveness of sins, the resurrection of the body, and life everlasting?**
  R. I do

Together:

Lord Jesus, I believe that you know me and love me. I have not always chosen to love you, and have broken my relationship with you through my sins. Thank you for proving your love for me on the cross so that our relationship can be restored.

I open the door of my heart and I invite you to be at the centre of my life—to be my Saviour and my Lord. Direct me and help me to live the Gospel with my whole life.

Our individual commitment to God is how we live out being a child of God. This moment of communal prayer shows us how we become brothers and sisters who are part of God's family, the Church. Our communal life as the Church is the completion of God's vision for his children to live as one universal family.

Going from here

The focus of *Discovery* has been to introduce you to the *kerygma*, the basic message of the Catholic faith, and to give you the opportunity to begin or renew your relationship with God. The journey doesn't end here! As we end this Faith Study, let's discuss where you will go from here in your relationship with God.

8 **What is one element of your relationship with God that you would like to improve in the next month? What steps can you take to make this improvement?**

Here are some practical steps to begin growing in your relationship with God:

- Talk to God every day through prayer.

- If you have not been baptized, talk to your group leader about pursuing baptism through a local RCIA (*Rite of Christian Initiation for Adults*) program.

- Read your Bible every day, beginning with the New Testament.

- Become involved in your local parish.

- Share your faith with others.

- Celebrate the Eucharist every Sunday.

- Go to Confession on a regular basis.

- Get to know the teachings of the Catholic Church, which can offer guidance on your journey with Jesus.

Summary

At some point, we all need to make a personal, adult decision about whether to embrace the relationship with God that he has offered to us. Jesus gives us the Holy Spirit and the guidance of the Church as sources of real help and grace that can be experienced individually and communally as we live this new life in him.

Living It Out

CHALLENGE

Foster your friendship with Jesus by taking time to pray and talk with him for at least 10 minutes every day. Foster your communal encounter with God by introducing yourself to someone at Sunday Mass.

MEMORIZE 2 CORINTHIANS 5:15

And he died for all, so that those who live might live no longer for themselves, but for him who died and was raised for them.

Appendix

Making a Good Confession

PRAYER BEFORE CONFESSION:

Oh most merciful God! Prostrate at your feet, I implore your forgiveness. I sincerely desire to leave all my evil ways and to confess my sins with all sincerity to you and through your priest. I am a sinner; have mercy on me, Oh Lord. Give me a lively faith and firm hope in the Passion of my Redeemer. Give me, for your mercy's sake, a sorrow for having offended so good a God. Mary, my mother, refuge of sinners, pray for me that I may make a good confession. Amen.

HOW TO GO TO CONFESSION:

- You have the option to go to confession anonymously (behind a screen) or face-to-face.

- After the priest greets you in the name of Christ, make the Sign of the Cross. He may choose to recite a reading from Scripture, after which you say, *"Bless me, Father, for I have sinned. It has been [state how long] since my last confession. These are my sins."*

- Tell your sins simply and honestly to the priest. You might even want to discuss the circumstances and the root causes of your sins and ask the priest for advice or direction.

- Listen to the advice the priest gives you and accept the penance from him. Then say an Act of Contrition for your sins. The priest will then absolve you of your sins and will pray the Prayer of Absolution. This prayer is a beautiful affirmation of God's mercy. Listen to its powerful words: *"God, the Father of mercies, through the death and resurrection of his Son has reconciled the world to himself and sent the Holy Spirit among us for the forgiveness of sins. Through the ministry of the Church may God give you pardon and peace, and I absolve you from your sins in the name of the Father, and of the Son, and of the Holy Spirit."*

- Afterwards, spend some time thanking and praising God for the gift of his mercy. Fulfill your penance as soon as possible.

ACT OF CONTRITION:

Oh my God, I am heartily sorry for having offended you and I detest all of my sins because of your just punishment, but most of all because they have offended you, my God, who are all good and deserving of all my love. I firmly resolve, with the help of your grace, to sin no more and avoid the near occasion of sin. Amen.

A simple prayer from the heart is also acceptable:

Lord, I am sorry for my sins. I thank you for your forgiveness, strength and love.

DO YOUR PENANCE:

When we go to Confession, we are cleansed and freed from our sins. Although the absolution we receive takes away the sin, it does not, however, remedy all the problems that sin causes. When we sin, we weaken ourselves as well as our relationship with God and our neighbours. We must repair the harm caused by our sin (e.g. return stolen goods or restore the reputation of someone about whom we have gossiped). That is why the priest gives us a penance.

The penance given usually depends on the gravity of the sin committed. Penances can consist of prayer, an offering, works of mercy, service to neighbour, voluntary self-denial, sacrifices, and above all the patient acceptance of suffering that brings us closer to Christ. The sacrament of Confession is not complete until you do your penance. It should be done immediately in the church, if it is a penance of prayer. Otherwise, it should be done as soon as possible.

EXAMINATION OF CONSCIENCE

I am the Lord your God, you shall have no other gods besides me.
Did I fail to love God, to make him first in my life, to thank, trust and love him as he deserves? Did I fail to pray? Have I doubted or denied my faith? Was I careless in saying my prayers? Do I give God time every day in prayer? Do I make a god out of my work, possessions, or image in the eyes of others so that these rule my life instead of God? Am I angry toward God because of illness or misfortune? Have I been involved with magic, horoscopes, Ouija boards or fortune telling?

You shall not take the name of the Lord your God in vain.
Did I curse or swear? Did I use God's name in vain, lightly, carelessly, by blasphemy? Have I used foul language or jokes? In conversation, have I passively listened to slander and to jokes demeaning the Church or God's authority?

Remember the Sabbath day, to keep it holy.
Have I deliberately missed Mass on Sundays or Holy Days of Obligation? Did I leave Mass early without good reason? Have I received communion at least once a year? Did I receive communion in a state of serious sin? Have I been to confession recently? In any of my previous confessions, did I lie to or deliberately conceal something from the priest? Have I allowed myself to become so dominated by my work and chores that I have not set aside Sunday for spiritual and family activities?

Honour your father and your mother.
Did I honour and obey my parents? Did I respect my brothers and sisters? Did I respect others with lawful authority, especially teachers and professors? Did I speak rudely to them? Did I speak about them to others in a derogatory way? Did I fail to help my parents (at home, or in their time of need)? Did I spend time with my family, or avoid them? Do I blame my parents for my own shortcomings?

You shall not kill.
Did I give in to feelings of anger or jealousy? Did I keep hatred in my heart? Have I ever struck anyone in anger, intending to injure the person? Did I fight, give a bad example or cause scandal? Have I abused alcohol or drugs? Have I had or in any way permitted or encouraged abortion? Have I nurtured thoughts about suicide?

You shall not commit adultery & you shall not covet your neighbour's wife.

Did I consent to impure glances or thoughts? Did I give my mind over to lustful thoughts or fantasies? Have I encouraged them by stares, curiosity or impure conversations? Did I neglect to control my imagination or desire of other people? Was I immodest in dress or behaviour? Did I look at pornography, impure books, magazines or videos? Am I guilty of impurity with myself, premarital sex or adultery? Do I live chastely according to my state in life (married, single, consecrated celibate)?

You shall not steal.

Have I stolen? What or how much? Did I return it or make up for what I stole? Have I cheated on tests or homework? Did I waste time at work? Did I do graffiti? Have I been extravagant in my manner of life, to the neglect of the poor at home and abroad?

You shall not bear false witness against your neighbour.

Have I lied, gossiped? Have I talked about other people behind their backs? Do I always tell the truth? Am I sincere? Did I reveal secrets that I should have kept confidential? Am I critical, negative or uncharitable in my talk? Have I injured the reputation of others by speaking about their failures and sins with little desire or intention to help them? Have I condoned prejudice and hatred toward people of other nationalities, races or religions?

You shall not covet your neighbour's goods.

Is my heart greedy? Am I jealous of what another has? Am I envious of others because I don't have what they have? Do I habitually compare myself with others? Do I work, study, and keep busy to counter idle thoughts? Am I critical, negative, or uncharitable in my thoughts of others? Is my heart set on earthly possessions or on the treasures of heaven? Do I give to those in need, so as not to cling to my possessions?

Your Feedback

Be part of the community of people who have participated in CCO faith studies. Let us know how you are growing as missionary disciples. Please give us your feedback by visiting **cco.ca/faithstudyfeedback.**

About CCO

Catholic Christian Outreach (CCO) is a university student movement dedicated to evangelization. We challenge young adults to live in the fullness of the Catholic faith with a strong emphasis on becoming leaders in the renewal of the world.

CCO's goal is to proclaim the gospel clearly and simply. We invite people to embrace a relationship with Christ, and we intentionally accompany them as they become *missionary disciples* and leaders in the New Evangelization.

Our primary ministry is on university campuses, where we reach out to students directly. CCO missionaries invite young adults to a relationship with Christ. We lead small group faith studies and host a variety of events, all designed to support each person's discipleship journey.

CCO hosts *Rise Up*, Canada's largest Catholic young adult conference in a major Canadian city each year. It brings together more than 800 young adults, inspiring and equipping them to lead evangelization efforts in their daily lives.

Catholic partners around the world invite CCO to host international and domestic missions. Mission participants are equipped to share CCO's evangelization methods, materials and approaches, collaborating with the local Church to clearly and simply share the Gospel message.

CCO began in 1988 at the University of Saskatchewan and now serves thousands of students on 16 campuses across Canada, has an active ministry in Uganda and collaborates closely with organizations throughout the Church. CCO's thriving staff team has grown to more than 100 missionaries.

CCO: Campus and more

MATERIALS

CCO's evangelization materials incorporate decades of ministry experience. These helpful tools, available in multiple languages, allow any missionary disciple to share the Gospel clearly and simply. In particular, the *Faith Study Series* facilitates intentional accompaniment through small group discussion, and the *Ultimate Relationship* booklet guides a brief kerygmatic conversation and invites the hearer to embrace a relationship with Christ.

CONNECT

Connect offers CCO's robust training and formation program to missionary disciple university students who want to reach out on their campuses. CCO missionaries accompany these student leaders, providing a remote experience modeled on the direct mentoring that happens on CCO campuses every day.

PARISHES

Parishes can benefit from CCO's 30 years of experience on the leading edge of evangelization; CCO's workshops and coaching have proven effective in transforming parish culture. Whether parishes are exploring options and want to test out some resources or are ready to commit to full-scale evangelization and discipleship efforts, CCO is ready to help.

ALUMNI

Are you a CCO alum? Join the CCO Alumni community for support, encouragement, fellowship and ongoing formation as you live out the mission in the world. Get connected at http://bit.ly/ccoalumni

Visit cco.ca

CCO Resources

There are many great programs for evangelization, yet CCO's Faith Study series is unique: it creates an environment for intentional accompaniment through personal relationships. The Faith Studies enable you to proclaim the Gospel message clearly and simply in a small group setting and equip your participants to become missionary disciples.

All our studies are available in English, French and Spanish. Some studies currently available in Chinese.

Level 1—*DISCOVERY* invites you to encounter Christ through a simple but challenging look at the Gospel message.

Level 2—*SOURCE* introduces you to the Holy Spirit and the impact that the third person of the Trinity can make in the lives of faithful Catholics.

Level 3—*GROWTH* examines the fundamental practices which nurture our Christian life such as prayer, sacraments and fellowship.

Level 4—*TRUST* deepens trust in God. This study helps participants grow in trusting the Lord in all aspects of life so as to live in greater freedom.

Level 5—*COMMISSION* focuses on revealing our missionary identity as Catholics and its necessity in approaching our apostolate and personal growth in holiness.

ORDER TODAY AT:
cco.ca/store

THE ULTIMATE RELATIONSHIP

The Ultimate Relationship booklet provides an easy way for anyone to share the Gospel message in a clear, simple and personal way. *The Ultimate Relationship* is currently available in nine languages, including English, French and Spanish.

CLEAR & SIMPLE

Clear & Simple goes beyond any particular evangelistic program to communicate the heart of relational ministry and care for souls: intentional spiritual conversations.

FORGIVENESS IS KEY

Through the pages of *Forgiveness Is Key*, God will draw you into his mercy and greater freedom.

5 TENETS TO RENEW THE WORLD

Five principles for evangelization that give you the building blocks for success.

CATHOLIC MISSIONARY IDENTITY

Presents a rediscovery of Catholic missionary identity as essential in order for the Church to experience renewal.

BRICK BY BRICK

With real life stories, tons of humour, and practical advice, this three-generation family illustrates seven key principles of discipleship parenting that bore great fruit raising their children to be missionary disciples.